G000068392

Your loved one has become more frail, forg
diagnosed with an illness or condition.

Your loved one can't work, or can't drive or can't cook, can't do the
housework or can't enjoy their hobbies.

It has become unsafe to leave your loved one on their own for any
length of time.

NOW, WHAT?

Who do I turn to?
Who do I ask?
How do I get a break?
My loved one needs care?
How will I afford it?

Handbook for carers who are facing, being or ending caring for someone they love.

How to get the best for your loved one.

Acknowledgements
Thank you to my wonderful husband, Jim. Thank you to my brilliant
mum Irene Watson, Peter Layland and Liz Gill for their advice and
support. Thank you to Danni Graham for lighting the spark inside me
and with Dee Burdett with the book title. Thank you to the carers
from Fuchsia Homecare that look after my husband.

I would like to explain why I decided to write this book. When my husband became ill, I didn't realise that I was becoming his carer. I thought I was doing my wifely duties.

In the beginning, it was very traumatic, emotional and overwhelming.

Illness has turned our lives upside down, our dreams smashed.

I had many enjoyable years as a professional carer. But this was definitely outside my experience or ability. I didn't know how to set up anything. As a professional carer, we are the last piece of a large jigsaw.

I did not realise at the start of the journey, how many professionals will be involved in my husband care and finally involved in my mental health care.

The following chapters include a checklist so you can keep track of who to contact, what to do and what to order.

It can be very confusing to know who does what, and what the terminology mean that they use. The terminology and the professionals roles are explained. Also I have included who you need to contact or be referred by to get a professional that you want. I hope I make a confusing time more clearer

Included are the websites and contact details for the relevant professionals and associations at the end of the chapter.

<u>Now I am a family carer, What now?</u>

4

5

1.RESPITE

Created by SBTS
from Noun Project

Checklist

Tasks	√	Tasks	√
Contact Social Services			
Contact Family Carer Association			
Contact the relevant association about the diagnosis			
Doctor surgery about carer respite services			
Social Worker			
Respite			
Hospice (Respite)			
Carer's direct helpline			
Plan things to do with your spare time			
Spend the money given by Social Service for you to pamper yourself			

Please look after yourself.

I heard a good story. The heart is extremely selfish and keeps all the richest nutritional blood for itself and then passes the remaining blood to the rest of the body. But if the heart fails, rest of the body dies.

Please look after your mental and physical health, pamper yourself regularly, keep a social life and use respite so you can get recharged. If you are ill or feeling under pressure, you can **request respite** and contact friends and Social Services to give you breathing space. Also, everything does not need to be perfect. If a person misses one meal out of 3 meals for the day or misses having personal care for 1 day and will get personal care from someone else the next day. Don't worry. The person will manage. Please look after yourself so you can look after the person with your full attention, love and care.

Respite is for the carer

Respite means NOT catching up on household duties.
Respite means NOT feeling guilty
Respite means getting out of the house
Respite means going shopping for enjoyment
Respite means getting pampered at the beautician
Respite means getting pampered at the barber

Respite means visiting friends
Respite means reading a book
Respite means going out for dinner
Respite means relaxing
Respite means doing your favourite hobbies
Respite means watching a move at home or at the cinema
Respite means catching up on TV
Respite means going to the pub
Respite means walking the dog
Respite means going fishing
Respite means going to a concert
Respite means going to festivals

You are not alone

Respite

Carers breaks are so you can look after your own health and well-being. You can ask your council or local carer's centre about respite in your area. Your carer's assessment may identify that you need a break from caring time to time. Read chapter two Finance about Care and Carer assessment

Social Services

Social service are the best people to contact initially. They can assist you with advice and with support. Please contact them before you start to feel overwhelmed and may have very negative thoughts about yourself or your loved one.

Family Carer Association

The Family carer association looks after the carer. They can provide counselling, respite, advice on issues that you are worried about and other services. You can search online or ask the Social worker for the Family carer association in your local area.

Association/Charity for the disease or condition of your loved one.

Please contact the association and they may be able to provide counselling, respite and more information about the disease or

Created by Alexandria Eddings from Noun Project

condition. There will be online support network that you can join for the extra support.

Doctor surgery

Let your doctor surgery know that you are a family carer. Your local GP may have services that give you extra support, such as coffee morning, counselling or a designated person to look after your health

Respite Holidays

You can have a holiday for yourself, or a holiday with your loved one in a specialist accommodation and you can relax while your loved one is being cared for or a holiday with your loved one.

Daycare centre

Your loved one can go to a daycare centre and stay for most of the day. Your loved one can meet other people, have a meal, do different activities and attend on full-time or part-time basis. You can ask the Social worker for more advice.

Domiciliary care

Carers can stay in the home with your loved one for an agreed time during the day while you get respite.

Respite care in care homes

Your loved one can stay in a residential care home for a short time and be looked after while you can recover from an illness, operation or you become unavailable. The residential care home can provide a room with en-suite, personal care, meal provided etc.

Please inform the care home of your loved one wishes about who to contact when they pass away and any other relevant information. If you are on holiday or unavailable.

Night Time Respite

You can get a full night sleep a few nights a week and some one stays awake all night and cares for your loved one. If your loved one has a terminal illness, care can be provided by Marie Curie or Macmillan. Please contact your District nurse for advice and support.

Carer's direct helpline

You can phone the carer's direct helpline if you need help with your caring role and want to talk to someone. If you want, you can text and ask an advisor to ring you at a time convenient to you.

Carer Assessment and may receive a one-off payment

Read chapter two Finance chapter for more information about the Carer and care assessment. You may receive a one-off amount of money to spend on yourself. The money is not to pay for carers. The money is for to you to spend on yourself, such as getting a haircut or paying for a housekeeper.

Contact details more information

Association	Contact Details
Social Services	www.nhs.uk/conditions/social-care-and-support
Family Carer Association	Search online for local Family carer association or ask the Social worker
Relevant Association for Diagnosis	Search online for the relevant association about the diagnosis
Doctor Surgery	Local Doctor Surgery
Respite	Local council
Respite centres	Look online and contact directly
Tourism for all	www.tourismforall.org.uk/
Revitalise	revitalise.org.uk/
The Disaway trust	www.disaway.co.uk
Holidays for All	www.holidaysforall.org/
DisabledGo	www.disabledgo.com/
Mindforyou	www.mindforyou.co.uk/
Calvert Trust	www.calvert-trust.org.uk/
Holiday Home trust	www.holidayhomestrust.info/
Disabled Holiday Directory	www.disabledholidays.com
Carers break in UK	https://www.carersuk.org/help-and-advice/health/looking-after-your-health/taking-a-break
Carer's Direct helpline	0300 123 1053 www.nhs.uk/conditions/social-care-and-support/carers-direct-helpline/

2.FINANCE

Checklist

Tasks	√	Tasks	√
Apply for Personal Independent Payment			
Carer Allowance			
Contact Social Services for a referral for the Benefit Advice Advisor			
Care and Carer assessment			
Blue Badge			
Mobility car			
Contact your Electricity company			
Contact the Council re Council Tax			
Contact the DWP re Housing Benefit			
Help with health costs			
NHS Continuing Healthcare			
Bereavement Payment			
Help from charities – Free services			
Help from charities - Grants			
Citizen Advice Bureau			

Attendance Allowance

Attendance allowance is for your loved one who is over 65 years old and physically or mentally disabled. The benefits do not cover mobility needs. You maybe able to claim for carer's allowance.

Personal Independent Payments

PIP is not based on the disability or the condition. It is based on the level of help your loved one needs. It doesn't matter if your loved one is working or not, have savings or not, will still receive PIP. There is 2 section- Daily Living rate and Mobility rate.

You maybe able to claim for carer's allowance.

14

Carer Allowance

You can receive carer allowance if you are looking after your loved one at least 35 hours a week and they are receiving certain benefit.

Benefit Advice Advisor

If you and your loved one is eligible. Ask the Social Worker for a referral to the Benefit Advice Advisor. The advisor can inform you of what benefit you can apply for.

Care and Carer Assessment

Ask the Social worker or Family Carer association for a "carer and care" assessment. It is an assessment of the needs of the carer and the needs of the person being looked after. So the correct services are being provided. Ask as soon as possible. It can take a long time to go through the process.

Blue Badge

You will need to apply to your local council for a Blue badge and find out if you qualify. Read chapter 9 Socializing outside the home for more information.

Created by Yu luck
from Noun Project

Mobility Car

If your loved one is receiving Personal Independent Payment Mobility allowance.

Your loved one may be eligible for a mobility car. The road tax, MOT is reduced and the car is suitable for the person with a disability to use. Cars are available in small or large size with a ramp or without.

Electricity Company

Let your electric company know that a disabled person lives in the home. If there is a power cut out, the company will make sure you are a priority.

Council Tax

Let the council be aware, that a disabled person lives at the address. You may be able to get the council tax reduced.

Housing Benefits

If you had to give up your job or the finances are being stretched. Can ask the Department Work and Pension for housing benefit. It depends on your circumstances.

Help with Health cost

You can claim for help with health cost if your loved one's savings is under a certain amount. You can ask the Social Worker or the Benefit Advice Advisor for assistance. Also can apply online.

Health Charges

You can ask the Social Worker or Benefit Advice Advisor to assist you or apply online. You may be able to receive the following for free or at a reduced amount if your loved one is eligible.

NHS Dental Services-search online for an NHS Dentist. Most Dentists have private and NHS clients. Please let the receptionist know that your loved one wants an NHS Dentist. You may need show proof of NHS entitlement. Treatment available on NHS crown and bridges, dental abscesses, denture (false teeth), orthodontics, root canal treatment, scale and polish, wisdom teeth, white fillings. The Dentist should have information at the clinic about what is available on the NHS. Your loved one needs to be aware before starting treatment if the Dentist is providing it privately or on the NHS.

Optical

The NHS eye test is free of charge if your loved one is in the eligible group or sight test is considered clinically necessary. Your loved one may be eligible for optical vouchers which contribute to buying glasses or contact lenses.

Travel charges

Your loved one can claim travel cost if on a low income and have made an additional journey to receive NHS care following a referral by a Doctor, GP or Hospital Doctor, Optician or Dentist. You will need to claim within 3 months from the date of the charges.

Wigs and fabric support

Your loved one maybe entitled to it free, need to show proof of entitlement or a war pension exemption certificate. Your loved one might be entitled to help with charges if you have a valid HC3 certificate

Prescription

If your loved one is eligible, may be able to get a free prescription. The medicines prescribed from a hospital or walk in clinic, prescribed contraceptives, medicines personally prescribed by a GP and medicines

supplied at a hospital or clinic commissioning group, or clinic for sexually transmitted infection, tuberculosis or a mental disorder that is subjected to a supervised community treatment order are FREE. The prescription prepayment certificate allows your loved one to save money on NHS prescription costs. The certificate allows your loved one to obtain all the prescriptions they need for £2 a week.

Continuing Healthcare

Please ask your Social worker about Continuing healthcare. If your loved one has a long term complex heath need may qualify for free social care. It can be provided in a variety of settings outside the hospital, such as in your home or in a registered care home. The Initial checklist assessment can be completed by a nurse, doctor, other healthcare professional or social worker. If your loved one meets the criteria for a full assessment, then a multidisciplinary team made up of a minimum of 2 health or care professionals will do a full NHS continuing healthcare assessment. If your loved one passes the assessment. Then a care and support package that meet your assessed needs will be arranged.

Bereavement Payment

If you are eligible, you may be able to claim the bereavement payment up to 12 months after your husband, wife or civil partner dies. Contact DWP to apply.

Help from charities

You may receive support, advice, counselling and practical help from charities for free, such as Marie Curie, Sue Ryder or a local hospice.

Grants from charities

You maybe able to apply for grants from Macmillan grants or Turn2us grant search. Contact CAB for more information.

Citizen Advice Bureau

You can get financial advice and support from the CAB. (Citizen Advice Bureau)

Forms Health

HC1(SC)

Claim for help with health cost

HC3

certificate for partial help with health costs

HC5

HC5 (D)Claim dental charges

HC5 (O)Claim Optical charges

HC5 (T)Claim travel charges

HC5 (W)Claim wigs and Fabric support

HC12

A quick guide to help with health costs including charges and optical voucher values

Contact details for more information

Association	Contact details
Personal Independent Payment	gov./pip/how-to-claim 08001214433
Attendance Allowance	www.gov.uk/attendance-allowance
Carer Allowance	www.gov.uk/carers-allowance/how-to-claim

Social Services	www.nhs.uk/conditions/social-care-and-support or Contact your local authority
Family Carer Association	Search online for local Family carer association or ask at Doctor Surgery
Blue Badge	www.gov.uk/apply-blue-badge
Mobility car	www.motability.co.uk
Electric Company	
Local Council	www.gov.uk/apply-for-council-tax-discount
Department of Work and Pension	
Help with Health cost helpline	0300 330 1343 www.nhs.uk/usng-the-nhs
Dental Service Helpline	0300 330 1348
Low Income Scheme helpline	0300 330 1343
Queries about medical exemption certificates	0300 330 1341 www.nhs.uk/usng-the-nhs
Queries about prescription Prepayment Certificates	0300 330 1341
Prescription service helpline	0300 330 1349
Queries about Tax credit certificate	0300 330 1347 www.nhs.uk/usng-the-nhs
Order paper copy of HC12, HC5,HC1(SC) forms	0300 123 0849
For all other queries call	0300 330 1343
Social Worker	
Beacon give free independent advice on NHS continuing healthcare	www.beaconchc.co.uk free helpline 0345 548 0300
Bereavement Payment	Contact your local Job Centre DWP.
Help from charities – Free services	Contact Marie Curie, Sue Ryder, Maggie's centres or local hospice
Help from charities – Grants Macmillan grants Turn2us grant search	https://www.macmillan.org.uk/information-and-support/organising/benefits-and-financial-support/benefits-and-your-rights/macmillan-grants. https://www.turn2us.org.uk/Get-Support
Citizen Advice Bureau	https://www.citizensadvice.org.uk/

3.PERSONAL CARE

Created by Luis Prado
from Noun Project

Checklist

Tasks	√	Tasks	√
Online shops for miscellaneous things			
Ready meals			
Food Shopping			
Dietician (Doctor referral)			
Clothes			
Hairdresser/Barber			
Social Worker			
District Nurse			
Incontinence Care (Doctor referral)			
Dentist			
Optician			
Chiropodist, Podiatrist Privately or NHS			
Manual and Positioning training			

Adult pads/Absorbent sheets

You can buy adult pads from all major stores and chemist. You can take them off by ripping the sides off the pad when it is on the person You can buy from Amazon, Ebay and other online shops, chemist (pharmacist) and all major stores. Some chemist will deliver adults pads with the prescription. Some major stores such as ASDA, Sainsbury, Morrison, Tesco and Waitrose may deliver to the home address.

Bed – buy disposable incontinent sheets or training pads to place on the bed and use once and throw away or use an Absorbent Incontinent sheet(Kylie) that can be washed regularly and tucked into the bed. They absorb a lot of liquid and keep the person and surrounding area dry.

Manual Wheelchair, Recliner or chair – The disposable incontinent sheet or absorbent incontinent sheet can be placed on the chair, recliner or wheelchair and keep your loved one dry.

22

Incontinence provisioned needed to look after your loved one.

Created by Kick
from Noun Project

-disposable incontinent sheets or Absorbent incontinent sheet.

-plastic bags for the carers to put in their apron, gloves, dirty pads, incontinent sheets, wet wipes and/or convene and day/night bags.

-toilet roll

-disposable gloves ask District Nurse.

-antibacterial hand washable

Personal care provisions needed to look after your loved one

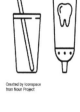

Created by Iconspace
from Noun Project

-Baby wipes

-2 flannels of different colours
 red-body, blue- private area.

-Body soap

-Shampoo/Conditioner

-Razor and Shaving cream

-Comb/Brush

-Toothpaste and Toothbrush

-Aftershave or Perfume

-Deodorant

-Creams

-Washing up bowl for bed bath.

-2 small towels

-1 large towel

-Make up

The items need to be next or near the person that is being washed.

Clothes

If it becoming more stressful and difficult to get your loved one dressed in the morning. You can search online for Adaptive clothing. The clothes are designed for getting on and off easier. The clothes are created for people in wheelchairs, elderly people and others with a wide range of medical conditions. Also if your loved one has gained weight or lost. You can buy clothes from charity shops and the major grocery shops.

Dressing

To dress your loved one that is immobile or with restricted movement. Remember to put the shirt on their weakest side first and take off weak side last. It is easier to put the arm in the sleeve by moving sideways in front of the body. When putting on trousers or jeans, gently move the ankle section of trousers near the knees and then pull up to the waist. It is easier to put the skirt/dress over the lady's head if they prefer not to lift their feet or are in a sitting position. Put the trousers, socks and shoe on the same leg at the same time, so your loved one lift their leg once. If the person is getting dressed while lying down in bed. Please be aware that it may hurt your loved one every time they are rolled from side to side on the bed. Please try to do everything with the minimum rolls.

Bed Bath (body wash in bed)

To give your loved one a bed bath quickly and thoroughly, it can be done by 1 or 2 people. Use 2 flannels with different colours. 1 flannel used for the body and face. The other flannel used for the private areas only. It reduces cross contamination. The upper body can be washed, dried, checked for bed sores, bruises and  dressed. Then it repeated on the lower body. If you notice any bed sores or bruises please let the District nurses know.

Wet Shave

it is easier to put a wet hot flannel on the area you will shave first. Put a towel around the shoulder and use a bowl of hot/warm water. Lather lots of shaving cream and apply to the face. Ask the person or ask a male that you know how they shave. Wipe the razor on your palm in the opposite direction. It will remove the hair from the razor while you giving a shave. If it start to catch the hair while shaving on the face or starts to hurt the person. You will need to replace the

24

blade. Wash off remaining cream, apply aftershave. Rinse razor under the tap when finished.

Hairdresser/Barber

Hairdressers are happy to wash your loved one's hair regularly at the salon or at home. Barbers are happy to shave men regularly.

Hair Wash

You can use a wet flannel to wet short hair as a temporary measure. Professional carers will wash your loved one hair.

Social Worker

If your loved ones want a bath and their home is not suitable or don't have one. You can ask the Social worker to find a bath with or without a hoist in the community.

Created by Eqquindi from Noun Project

District Nurse

District nurses are available 24 hours for home visits and/or advice.

District nurses can provide advice, support and aids that can make life easier such as items to put on the bed to reduce the possibility of getting bed sores or helping to reduce them. Read chapter 4 Health

Incontinence care

The Continence Nurse can provide things like adult pads, catheters and male and female urinal bottles, sheath and appliances to assist your loved one. For more information see chapter 4 Health

Commode (toilet chair)

Can be used on it own or will go over a toilet.

Manual and Positioning

If you need to move someone, please contact Social Service and request an Occupational Therapist (OT) to visit and can provide Moving and Positioning training if you want. The professional carers are trained to move people safely. The OT can provide equipment such as banana board and sliding sheets or if the person can't stand up. The OT may provide a hoist (lifting equipment) which will transfer a person from one location to another. Please speak to the OT for more information.

Drinking

You can put a hot/warm drink and a cold drink beside your loved one so they have a choice and are always hydrated.

Dehydration

Dehydration is not what you want. To find out if your loved one is dehydrated or not. You can lightly pinch the skin between thumb and finger. If it springs back slowly, it may mean your loved one is dehydrated. Your loved one will need to drink more liquids

Dietician.

If you loved one eating habits have changed or are changing. You can request a dietician to visit. Read chapter 4 Health.

Ready Meals

You can have Ready meals delivered by specialized companies to your home and put in the freezer. The meals can be reheated in the oven or microwave by your loved one or the carers. All diet requirements are covered.

Food Shopping

Can order food shopping by most major shops online and be delivered to their home.

Dentist

If your loved one can't attend the Dentist in person. You can ask your Dentist for a referral to a Specialist Dental Service. Community Dental services are available in a variety of places to ensure everyone can have access to dental health. These include hospitals, specialist health centres, mobile clinics, home visit or visits in nursing homes and care homes.

Optician

Free NHS eye test and voucher. Read chapter 2 Finance.

Chiropodist, Podiatrist

National Institute for Health and Care Excellence (NICE) recommends that Foot care services should be provided on NHS for long term conditions such as Diabetes, Peripheral Arterial disease and rheumatoid arthritis. You will need to ask your GP if you qualify for NHS podiatry treatment. If not, you can have private treatment and some do home visit.

Legality of a Family carer.

Family carers, as far as I know, don't need to abide by any laws. As a general rule, the professional involved in your loved one care can give you advice and suggestions. Please look after your back. You may move your loved one with or without a hoist in your own home, maybe safe or unsafe manoeuvre. It is yours and your loved one decision to accept the risk. The professional that may visit your home has to follow their company policy and the law.

Contact details for more information

Association	Contact details
Dietician	
Ready meals	Search online for Ready meals that are delivered
Social Worker	www.nhs.uk/conditions/social-care-and-support or Contact your Local authority
Hairdresser/Barber	
Continence Nurse Bladder and Bowel Nurse	01616078219 https://www.bbuk.org.uk/
District Nurse	Contact your local GP surgery
Dentist	Local Community Dental care. Contact NHS England 0300 311 2233
Optician	
Chiropodist/Podiatrist	NHS-www.nhs.uk/live-well/healthy-body/foot-problems Private Chiropodist or Podiatrist www.nhs/uk/service-search/podiatrist

4.HEALTH

Created by Arafat Uddin
from Noun Project

Checklist

Tasks	√	Tasks	√
GP - Visit surgery or home visit			
Keep in contact with Doctor surgery regularly			
Carer support from surgery			
Chemist/Pharmacy			
Specialist			
District Nurse			
Occupational Therapist			
Physiotherapist			
Dietician			
Continence nurse (Bladder and Bowel nurse)			

GP surgery

The GP surgery has lots of services available. Let them know that you are a family carer. The surgery maybe able to give you extra support and advice.

Dossett/Blister Pack and Delivery

You can ask the chemist/pharmacy to put the medication prescribed into a dossett box/blister pack – possibly there may be with a small charge or fee to have these boxes filled and delivered. That way, you know when the medication is to be administered and if taken.

If the doctor makes any amendments, the chemist will make the necessary change.

Unused Medication

Please take unwanted medication to the chemist, they will dispose of it safely. That way, no mistakes, overdoses and children can't take them by mistake.

Administering

As a Family Carer, you are not restricted by law. You can administer prescribed drugs and home remedies drugs to your loved one. Professional carers have to abide by law and company policies about administering medication. Carers can only administer medication that is prescribed by the GP and Specialist, not home remedies. The medication has to have a label with your loved one name, name of medication, dosage, time and frequency, how to be taken e.g. by mouth, tablet or liquid. Home remedies are medication bought at a chemist without prescription or family remedies for illness.

Refusing

If your loved one is refusing the medication. You can ask your GP and Specialist to look at alternative ways of treatment or administer the drugs into a different form. Eg change from tablet to liquid. Please do not add medication to food or drink unless agreed by the GP or Specialist. Your loved one has to understand why and accept. Your loved one has the right to refuse. Please let your GP or Specialist be aware.

Re-order

If you need to re-order existing medication and don't have a repeat prescription. You can add to the bottom of an existing prescription.

Created by Linseed Studio
from Noun Project

Amendments

You can ask the Doctor to amend the administration times so it will suit your loved one. It does not need to be administered at 7am if your loved one is asleep. The doctor can prescribe a later time to suit your loved one routine. The doctor can be flexible with administration times.

31

Side effects
Please read the information sheet that is in the medication box about side effects. If concern about any changes physically or mentally. Please let the District nurse or Doctor be aware.

PRN
The doctor can prescribe PRN (PRN means "when required") that is separate from the blister, dossett box. PRN medication can be pain relief or medication that is administered for other reasons.

Vomiting, Diarrhoea, Constipation
If your loved one feels like he/she want to vomit or has difficulty going to the toilet or going too often. Please let your doctor be aware. The doctor can administer medication to assist and make your loved one feel better. You can place a plastic bag to line the Kitty litter tray and add toilet paper or kitchen roll to absorb the liquid at the bottom. If the person has the bowl in the bed while sleeping and knocks it over. The liquid will stay in bowl.

District Nurse
Available for advice and support and home visits
7 days a week, 24 hours
The District nurses work in the community and visit people in their homes. District Nurse can provide support and advice about medication that the doctor has prescribed to your loved one, about catheters and continence care and refer your loved one to Continence nurse if required, can treat bed sores, wounds and administer complex medication. District nurse can refer your loved one to another professional. If you have any concerns or worry about what to do or concern about the different health issues, contact the District nurse

Created by arif fajar yulianto from Noun Project

Bed Sores/Bed Ulcers
If you notice that your loved one is sitting or sleeping in one position for a long time. You can try to get your loved one to move or you move your loved one to a different position. It only needs to be a few

inches. So the blood can flow back to the area. If your loved one says that an area hurts, move as soon as possible. It may reduce the possibility of a bed sore forming. You will notice slight red marks at first, it will become more pronounced. You will need to contact the District nurse as soon as possible. If left untreated can turn into a bed sore/bed ulcer which can lead to sepsis. It is very difficult to get rid of. You can put one pillow length way under one leg so the heel is off the bed and the same on the other legs. Bed sores tend to occur on the bottom, elbows and heels and on areas where your loved one hasn't moved.

Occupational Therapist (OT)

You will need to ask your GP for a referral to the Occupational Therapy. Your loved one may get the OT free through NHS or Social services but depends on your circumstances.

The OT aims is to improve your loved one ability to do everyday tasks if they find it difficult.

Physiotherapist

You will need to ask your GP for a referral. Some Doctor surgery allows self-referral. Your loved one can go privately or NHS. Physiotherapy can help your loved one with education and advice, daily exercises and manual therapy.

Swallowing problems

If you are concerned that your loved one is having difficulty swallowing. Please let your GP or District Nurse know. They will refer you to the relevant professional and have treatment.

Dietician

If your loved one is not eating and you are getting concerned, you can contact their GP's and get a referral to a Dietician. The Dietician can give you suggestions, support and supplements. While you are waiting for the Dietician appointment, you can ask the Pharmacist (Chemist) for advice. Also, you can buy energy drinks,

Created by Nithinan Tatah
from Noun Project

energy bars and meal replacements drinks from all the major grocery shops and chemists.

Malnourishment

If your loved one is losing weight without a reason, low body weight, lack of interest in eating and drinking, feeling tired all the time, feeling weaker, getting ill often and slow to recover. Your loved one may be malnourished. Please tell your local GP or District Nurse about your concerns.

Dehydration

A general indicator. If the urine is dark yellow it may mean that the person is dehydrated and may need more liquids to drink. If the urine is a pale colour it may mean that the person is drinking plenty of liquids.If concerned, contact Doctor surgery or District nurse.

Eye drops, Nose drops, Ear drops

Created by Llisole from Noun Project

Can buy eye, nose and ear drops from the chemist/pharmacist without a prescription. You can ask the chemist for advice on how to administer the drops safely. When wiping the eyes, use 1 tissue for the left eye and another tissue for the right eye. It reduces cross contamination.

Cream

The label on the cream need to have your loved one name, how to be applied, dosage, how often and date then the carer can use it. Cream canesten, E45, pro-shield, conotrane and more.

Urine sample

If you think your loved one has an infection or your GP has requested an urine sample. The easiest way is to ask the Doctor surgery for a cardboard bowl and place it in the toilet. You can get a sample from the commode bowl after the person is finished on the commode.

Continence nurse (Bladder and Bowel nurse)

If your loved one is having difficulty using the toilet. You can ask the GP or District nurse to be referred to the Continence nurse (Bladder and Bowel nurse). You can also do a self referral to the Continence

Nurse. They can help with strategist and aids to help. Things like adult pads, catheters and male and female urinal bottles, sheath and appliances.

999

If your loved one is seriously ill or injured and their life is at risk. PHONE 999

How to contact 999 for Deaf people

You can contact 999 by texting. You will need to register your phone. Text "register" and send to 999, they will reply with a message about the service, read and reply "yes", receive another text to say that you are registered.

Information needed in a text

do you want fire or police or ambulance

what happening, briefly.

Where help needed- full address, landmark. Easier for fireman, ambulance or police to find you.

111

If you are worried about your loved one. You can phone 111 and talk with a trained advisor. "They will ask questions to assess your symptoms and, depending on the situation, will then; give self-care advice, connect you to a nurse, emergency dentist or GP, book a face to face appointment, send an ambulance if necessary and direct you to the local service that can help you best with your concerns." quote from www.nhs.uk "How does NHS 111 work?

How to contact 111 for Deaf people

You can contact 111 by using "**Interpreternow**" on the computer, tablet or phone app

111 online

If you have a question about your loved one or your self. It can answer questions, give advice, find out where to go for assistance, get a call back from a nurse, find out what to do if you can't see your usual doctor or dentist.

Typetalk or Textphone

To use the textphone by calling 18001 111.

Contact details for more information

Association	Contact details
Local Doctor surgery/GP	
Local Chemist/Pharmacy	
Specialist	
District Nurse	
Carer Support from surgery	
Occupational Therapist	
Sepsis more information	www.nhs.uk/conditions/sepsis/
Physiotherapist	
Nutritionist/Dietician	
Incontinent nurse (Bladder and Bowel)	01616078219 https://www.bbuk.org.uk/
999 nine, nine, nine	Emergency
999 Deaf	Text to 999. need to register first.
111 one, one, one	Free NHS helpline service for urgent medical concerns
111 Deaf	Interpreternow.co.uk/nhs111
111 online	111.nhs.uk/

5.HOSPITAL

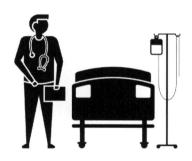

Created by Vectors Market
from Noun Project

Checklist

Tasks	√	Tasks	√
P.A.L.S			
Organise someone to push my loved one in a wheelchair, if available.			
Ward Nurse			
Contact Hospital Family Carer			
Non-emergency patient transport			
Refund Transport costs			
Contact existing care company to let them know your loved one is admitted to hospital			
Inform DWP PIP when your loved one is admitted and discharged			
Contact relevant people if your loved one can't attend an appointment.			

Hospital – The Occupational Therapist, Dietician, Social Worker, Physiotherapist and Family carers that are based in the hospital are separate to the community based professionals. In the hospital, the relevant professional will visit your loved one at their bedside.

P.A.L.S- Patient Advice and Liaison Service

It is a point of contact for you and your loved one while in the hospital. They can assist with any concerns and complaints about the NHS. Generally located near the front entrance.

Wheelchair use

If your loved one can walk, but finds walking around the hospital too difficult or walks too slow. You can drop off your loved one at the front and leave them in the wheelchair that is located in the entrance. Then park your car. You can push your loved one in a wheelchair to the relevant department. If you can't push the wheelchair, you can ask PALS or the reception desk for assistance. It may be a good idea to let the hospital know that you may need assistance with pushing your loved one when you confirm the appointment. They can give you advice or organise something.

38

Ward Nurse (Family carer pack)

You can ask the Ward nurse about the Family carer pack if it available.

Family and Carer Support

When your loved one is admitted into the hospital. Please let the hospital know that you are a Family carer. The family and carer support worker can support you and give advice.

Discharged from hospital

Once the Doctor has said that your loved one can go home. The discharge assessment will be discussed with your loved one. With your loved one permission, you will be informed and can contribute. Each hospital has different discharge policy. You can ask PALS or Ward manager for a copy of the discharge policy.

Care and support plans

While in the hospital and before your loved one gets discharged. A care plan for your loved one and a support plan for you will be created. It will set out in detail the care and support needs outside the hospital.

Occupational Therapist

The OT aims is to improve your loved one ability to do everyday tasks if they find it difficult. The OT will discuss alternative ways doing things with your loved one before discharge.

Created by Gan Khoon Lay
from Noun Project

Physiotherapist

Physiotherapy can help your loved one with education and advice, daily exercises and manual therapy. The Physiotherapist will discuss exercises to do at home before discharge.

Dietician

If your loved one is having difficulty or refusing to eat while in hospital. The Dietician can discuss different options for your loved one while in hospital.

Family Carer Pack

If the person you are looking after is being admitted to West Suffolk Hospital (Bury St Edmunds) for an overnight stay or extended stay.

You can request a Family Carer Pack in the ward. You will be given a "Family Carer" badge, which means you can buy your meals from the Time Out restaurant on the First floor and pay concessionary rates. You will need to register as a family carer with the parking attendant so you can get the discount rate. I am not aware at this moment in time if other hospitals offer a similar scheme.

Non-emergency patient transport

Contact PALS or Hospital reception for the Non-emergency patient transport phone number. Non-emergency patient transport is available for people whose condition needs additional medical support or find it difficult to walk. It needs to be booked at least 2 days before the appointment. The carer or family member will need to find their own way to the hospital. It might not be available in all areas. To find out if your loved one can use the service. You will need to talk to your loved one GP or Healthcare professional that referred him/her.

Claim Travel costs

Travel charges

Read the Finance chapter for more information

Contact details for more information

Association	Contact details
PALS	Generally, near the front entrance, contact GP surgery or hospital or 111 for details on where to find one.
Family and carer support	Contact P.A.L.S or Ward Nurse
Non-emergency patient transport	Contact the hospital for contact details or GP or Health professional.
Claim travel costs order paper form - HC5(T)	0300 123 0849
Personal Independent Payment (PIP) Inform of admittance and discharge dates.	0800 121 4433

6.PROFESSIONAL CARER

Created by Luis Prado
from Noun Project

Checklist

Tasks	√	Tasks	√
Contact Social Worker			
Care Companies/Care Providers			
Care Quality Commission			
What is the best type of care that will suit our family			
NHS care			
Is my loved one being abused?			

Social Worker/ Social Services

If you need support or advice about the professional carers or other issues. Contact Social service immediately.

Professional carers

Can assist you and relieve the pressure of caring for your loved one full time. Professional carers can do personal care, administer medication, light housework, cooking, moving and positioning, laundry, petty cash, food shopping and other jobs.

Hospital Stay

When your loved one leaves the hospital, the hospital may provide carers for the short term at home. The hospital social worker will discuss the options before discharge.

Care Companies/Care Providers

The care companies are privately owned. Each care company will specialize in a different area. Their standard of care will vary from very poor to outstanding. You will need to find a care company that suits your loved one needs and wants.

Care Quality Commission CQC

All care providers that provide care in your home, community or residential homes are inspected by CQC and do regular inspections and unannounced inspections. You can see on the website if the company are good or bad or where they need to improve.

Changing Care Providers

If you are not happy with the care provided and after you have discusses the issues with the care provider and nothing improves. You can change the care provider/company to a different provider. You can look online or ask your Social Worker for advice and support. It doesn't matter if you are paying or the NHS.

Different type of Care

Domiciliary(Community care)- carer visits your loved one in their home and can assist with personal care, light household duties and other jobs. The visit is for a short time and vary in frequency

Live in carers-carer lives in the home over a length of time. Can assist your loved one in the night and day with personal care, housework and other jobs.

Abuse

If you have concerns that your loved one is being abused or you are not happy with the standard of care. Contact the manager at the care company immediately. It doesn't matter if it a small or large worry. The care manager can deal with it. If you are still not happy, the care company will have a complaint procedure. If you continue to have concerns, you can contact the CQC. If you are not sure what is abuse or how to spot it. You can find more information on the NHS website listed below.

Contact details for more information

Association	Contact details
Social Worker	www.nhs.uk/conditions/social-care-and-support or Contact your Local authority
Care Companies	
Care Quality Commission	Www.cqc.org.uk
Abuse Action on Elder abuse	www.nhs.uk/conditions/social-care-and-support/vulnerable-people-abuse-safeguarding/ 0808 8088141 www.elderabuse.org.uk

7.HOME

Created by anna kang
from Noun Project

Checklist

Tasks	√	Tasks	√
Social Worker			
Occupational Therapist			
GP			
Disability shops			
Contact Local council for housing if current accommodation not suitable			

Social Worker

The social worker can give you advice and support and refer you to the Occupational Therapist.

Occupational Therapist

Social service may provide the alarms for free after your loved one had an assessment from the OT or the local council should leave you enough money to buy the alarms after care support charges have been deducted. Your loved one will need to discuss it with Social services.

Telecare and alarms

The telecare and alarms can allow your loved one to live in their homes independently. There is a network of sensors in their homes and linked through the telephone. If something happens, it will trigger an alarm and contact you. So you can go over and check.

Telehealth systems

Telehealth can help your loved one to self-manage their health conditions. It intends to complement rather than replace traditional care. The devices are useful for people with heart conditions, chronic asthma, diabetes, lung problems or epilepsy.

Baby monitor

A useful piece of equipment. It can give you peace of mind while you are in another room.

Household equipment, aids and adaptions.

There is a huge range of aids and equipment available on NHS that can support your loved one to be more independent in their own home. Please contact your GP or Social worker for a referral for an Occupational Therapist. The OT can visit and assess their needs and provide your loved one with the relevant household equipment, aids and adaptions.

Disability shops

Disability shops are located all over the UK. They sell a range of mobility scooters, daily living aids and equipment, clothing and footwear, furniture, personal health and stairlifts. You can visit the shop and they can help in making your loved one life easier.

Council housing

If your loved one is renting and the accommodation is not suitable. You can contact the local council and request adaption to the house or move to a more suitable accommodation.

Contact details for more information

Association	Contact details
Social Worker	www.nhs.uk/conditions/social-care-and-support or Contact your Local authority
Occupational Therapist	
GP	
Disability shops	
Local council	

8.HOME HINTS AND TIPS FOR HOUSEWORK

Checklist

Tasks	√	Tasks	√
Shopping			
Contact Local Council for emptying rubbish bins			

Duvet cover - Duvet Burrito

Place the inside out duvet cover flat on the bed with the opening at the end of the bed. Place duvet flat on top of the duvet cover. Roll the duvet cover and duvet together from the top of the bed to bottom. Take the duvet cover that is on the bottom closest to mattress nearest to the corner and turn it inside out and at the same time put the duvet inside. Do the same on the other side. Then do up the buttons or zips and then roll it out fully on the bed. Search YouTube for Duvet Burrito.

Rice for a wet phone

If a remote control or mobile phone gets accidentally dropped in water separate the battery and back cover, place everything into a container full of rice and cover up. Leave for a few days and it will dry out

Bicarbonate Soda

It can be used to absorb unwanted smells. The bicarbonate soda can be sprinkled on to the carpet after being vacuumed. It can be put into bowls in the fridge and different rooms in the house. You can buy **cleaning** Bicarbonate of Soda or Baking Soda from some stores and online. Buy the Bicarbonate soda or Baking Soda for cleaning only. It looks different and cheaper than cooking Bicarbonate of soda and Baking Soda

Waste

Put 3 plastic bags into the kitchen rubbish bin. It is easier. If the 1st bag has a hole or contains liquid, the 2nd bag will contain it. The 3rd bag is there already in the bin to use.

Wheelie Bin

You can ask the local council if they have bins for waste collection of adults pads and related items.

Bedding

You can keep matching pillow case, duvet cover and sheet inside the matching pillow case. Everything is kept together and look neat.

Contact details for more information

Association	Contact details
YouTube	Search for duvet burrito
Online shopping	
Local Council _____	

9.SOCIALIZING OUTSIDE THE HOME

Created by Gan Khoon Lay
from Noun Project

Checklist

Tasks	√	Tasks	√
Apply for Blue badge			
Buy Radar key			
Red Cross			
Shopmobility			
Mobility car			
Spare clothes			
Bus pass			
Train card			
CEA Cinema Exhibitors Association card			

Blue Badge

You can park in Disabled parking for free or a reduced fee and park on double yellow line and other benefits. Read chapter two Finance.

Blue Badge Parking in Bury St Edmunds

Wherewow Guide includes shops and eateries within 30 steps from BLUE BADGE PARKING IN BURY ST EDMUNDS By Lyndie Dempsey On sale at wherewowwherewow.weebly.com or   lyndiedempsey.weebly.com

Radar key

Radar keys open Disabled toilets in the community. You may need to ask your local Tourist Information centre or Local Council on where to buy one. The cost is generally under £6.00.

Disabled Toilet/ Changing places

Disabled toilets are located in the majority of public places e.g. Pubs, restaurants and parks.

Changing places *toilets* are located all over the U.K.

You will need to have a search on Changing places website to find the closest changing place toilet to you. The changing places toilets have height adjustable tables, more room to manoeuvre and ceiling hoist.

Red Cross

You can hire a manual wheelchair from the Red Cross. Please be aware that they are open on certain days and certain times. Search your local Red Cross online.

Shopmobility

You can hire wheelchairs and mobility scooters to use for the day, evening or for several days for a small charge. You will need to fill in an application form and show your loved one identification. Some shopmobility may require that your loved one has lessons on how to use the scooter.

Created by Nick abraham
from Noun Project

Major Shops – Free wheelchair hire

All major shopping outlets and large gardening centres have free wheelchairs and scooters near the front door to use. Be aware. They have an alarm attached to them. So when you take the wheelchair out to get the person from the car, the alarm may go off. Don't worry. The security is aware of it.

Mobility car

If your loved one is receiving Personal Independent Payment Mobility allowance. Your loved one may be eligible for a mobility car. The road tax, MOT is reduced and the car is suitable for the person with a disability to use. Cars are available in small or large size with a ramp or without.

Spare bag of Clothes

it is always a good idea, to take a bag of spare clothes when going out in the community and which can be kept in the car if unforeseen accidents happen.

How to fold and unfold a manual wheelchair.
How to push a manual wheelchair

ALWAYS USE THE BRAKES!

- Always put the brakes on before trying any of the tasks described below.

Opening the wheelchair

- Stand in front of, or to the side of the chair.
- Push armrests as far apart as possible.
- Push down on the side edges of the seat to ensure it is fully open, keeping your fingers pointing inwards to avoid them being trapped.

Closing the Wheelchair

- Lift the footplates upright and footrests out to the side, or remove completely.
- Stand beside the chair.
- Hold the middle of the seat canvas at the front and back.
- Give a sharp pull upwards and lift until the chair is fully closed.

- Store the wheelchair with the canvas pulled up, not tucked inside.

Getting out of the wheelchair

- Apply the brakes.
- Release the lap strap (if used).
- Lift the footplates upright or completely remove (never step on the footplate while getting out of or sitting down on the wheelchair as this can cause it to tip).
- Put your hands on the armrests and, keeping your feet slightly apart, slowly push yourself up.

Going down a kerb
(guidelines for attendant)

Backwards (easier, to lower the chair gently, but can be more dangerous because your back is to traffic).

- Look for a ramp or dropped kerb. If none is available:
- Ensure the chair is backwards to the kerb and square to it.
- Pull back and down on chair handles and push one foot down on the tipping lever until front castors lift (*right*).
- Ensure road is clear by following Highway Code procedure.
- Move backwards into road and gently lower the chair's rear wheels over the kerb onto the road, keeping castors tilted.
- Once rear wheels are on road, pull chair backwards until castors are clear of kerb.
- Lower castors to the road.

Forwards

- As above, but ensure the chair is facing forward and square to the kerb and, once rear wheels are on the road, lower the castors.

Going up a kerb

- Position chair square to kerb.
- Pull back and down on chair handles and push one foot down on the tipping lever until front castors lift.
- Move forward so front wheels are over pavement.
- Lower front wheels and lift back wheels over kerb.

How to put in a boot of a car.

Putting the wheelchair in a car boot

- Apply the brakes.
- Remove accessories—strap, cushions, armrests, footrests, etc (see below).
- Close the chair (bungee elastic could be helpful to stop chair opening again when lifting).
- Place chair parallel to car boot.
- Bend your knees, keep your back straight, grip the frame.
- Lift the chair to balance it on the lip of the boot (a piece of carpet or similar maybe helpful to protect car here) and then slide it carefully in.
- To get the chair out again, use the reverse process to the one described above.

Removing Footrests
(if relevant)

- Push plate A towards the back of the chair to release catch.
- Swing footrest out.
- Grasp at point B and lift to remove.

Removing Armrests
(if relevant)

- Pull lever at A.
Lift armrest up and out of sockets

Folding Backrests

- Stand behind the chair and lift level B
- Pull handles backwards.
Reverse the above procedures to re-install the components.

Bus Pass

The bus fare is free or is reduced. Most buses are wheelchair friendly. Please check with the bus company beforehand.

Disabled Person Railcard

The train fares are reduced for the disabled person and carer.

Not all train station is suitable for wheelchairs. Please check on the train station website before starting your journey. If you need assistance to get off or on the train due to mobility issue or visual impaired. Please contact the train station before arriving for the train.

Cinema Exhibitors card.

When you go to the cinema. Show the CEA card and pay for one person and the second person is free. You will need to fill in an application form online or at the cinema.

Local cinema for people with sensory loss.

Show movies with audio description and subtitles.

Signed performance in Theatre

Signed, captioned, Integrated performance all over the UK.

Sport for people with disability

Can find a sport that your loved one can play and is local.

Attractions – free for carers

When you are visiting a tourist attraction such as the Zoo, your loved one can go in on a concessionary rate. Some attractions allow the carer in for FREE or at a reduced rate. Ask at the ticket office.

Disabled Taxi

Disabled taxi can be hailed from a Taxi rank or booked by phone. The wheelchair access taxi has a ramp for easy access. So the person can stay sitting in the wheelchair or sit in the taxi seat.

Urine bottle

While you are out and your loved one has used the urine bottle. You can put the urine bottle in a toilet with the opening under the jet of water. Flush the toilet and it will rinse the bottle. It will not get flushed, because it is too big.

Contact details for more information

Association	Contact details
Blue Badge	www.gov.uk/apply-blue-badge and local council
Local Council	
Radar key	www.radarkey.org
Tourist Information centre	
Changing rooms	http://changingplaces.uktoiletmap.org/
Red Cross	www.redcross.org.uk/get-help/borrow-a-wheelchair
Shopmobility	www.shopmobility.org.uk/
Mobility car	www.motability.co.uk/
Bus pass	www.gov.uk/apply-for-disabled-bus-pass
Disabled Person Railcard	www.disabledpersons-railcard.co.uk/using-your-railcard/how-to-apply
National Railcard	www.railcard.co.uk
Traveline	Www.traveline.info/.
Sustrans for NCN routes and cycling	www.sustrans.org.uk
Taxi from train station	www.traintaxi.co.uk
Cinema Exhibitors Association card	www.ceacard.co.uk
Movies with subtitles and Audio	www.yourlocalcinema.com
Theatre London and in UK	www.officiallondontheatre.co.uk/access/signed
English Federation of Disability Sport	www.efds.co.uk
Support through Sport	http://supportthrough.co.uk

10.TRAVELLING IN THE UK AND ABROAD

Created by Tran
from Noun Project

Checklist

Tasks	√	Tasks	√
Local		Overseas	
Book accommodation		Book accommodation	
Book travel plane, train, ferry, car		Book travel plane, train ferry, car	
Contact GP for medication		Contact GP for medication	
Contact airport		Contact airport	
		Passport valid	
		Visa required?	
		Travel insurance	
		Organize blue badge to use overseas	
Mobility equipment hire UK		Mobility equipment hire overseas	
		Apply for European Health Insurance card (EHIC) E111.	
		Bring EHIC card	

Stockpiling Medication

If you are going on holiday and need to order extra medication. Please let the GP and the pharmacy know approx 8 weeks beforehand.

Bringing medication with you overseas

1. *Check with each country that you are passing through and visiting.*
2. *Check the type of medicine they allow to be taken into the country*
3. *Check the maximum quantity you can take in*

DON'T ASSUME THAT YOUR MEDICATIONS WILL BE ACCEPTED.

Please keep the medication and medical equipment such as needles, syringes in their original packets. So the airport security and customs know that it belongs to you. Carry your medication and a copy of the prescription, Doctor letter in your hand luggage and a spare supply of medication and a copy of your prescription, Doctor letter in a suitcase. In case you lose your hand luggage or suitcase. Please check with airline's regulations before travelling.

VERY IMPORTANT

You will need a Doctor letter stating the details of your medication, including generic name, the name of the health condition that you need the medication for. Suggestion- it may be a good idea to get the information translated into the language of the country you visit. Be aware that you may be charged by the GP surgery for writing of the letter.

Special Assistance at Airports in UK and Abroad

As a general rule, the airline is responsible for providing assistance. Let the airline know as soon as possible about the disability. For more information, look online for "special assistance" at the airport that you and your loved one are departing from.

How to request a wheelchair or cart at the airport.

After you have booked the tickets, contact the airline and request a wheelchair or cart to meet your loved one off at the plane.

Travel insurance

Make sure that the travel insurance covers your loved one while overseas. Check the small print.

How, when and where to use Blue badge in Europe

The leaflet from the AA contains a translation for each country, which can be printed out and displayed with your badge. It explained in their own language that you and your loved one are foreign visitors, you have the same concessions as the local disabled people and the parking is legal. The image is taken from the AA website.

Mobility equipment hire UK and overseas

Can search online and find companies that will hire hoists, commodes, wheelchairs and other equipment that is needed to enjoy your holiday in the UK or abroad.

European Health Insurance

"The European Health Insurance card can be used to cover any necessary medical treatment due to either an accident or illness within the European Economic area. The EHIC entitles the holder to state-provided medical treatment within the country they are visiting and the service provided will be the same as received by a person covered by the country's insured medical scheme."

Quote from www.e111.org.uk

Contact details for more information

Local travel	Contact details (Local)	Overseas Travel	Contact details (Overseas
GP surgery _____			
Airport _____		Airport _____	
Train _____	impersonalisation-railcard.co.uk/using-your-railcard/how-to-apply	Train _____	
Ferry Terminal _____		Ferry _____	
Passport	https://www.gov.uk/government/organisations/hm-passport-office	Visa	
Travel Insurance		Travel Insurance _____	
		Blue badge overseas	www.theaa.com/public_affairs/reports/blue_badge_abroad.pdf
Mobilty equipment hire UK	Search online	Mobility equipment hire overseas	Search online
Car hire _____		Car hire _____	
Local Bus _____	www.gov.uk/apply-for-disabled-bus-pass	Local bus _____	

64

Local Taxi		Local Taxi	
NHS healthcare	NHS	Apply for Free European Health insurance card	www.nhs.uk/using-the-nhs/healthcare-abroad/apply-for-a-free-ehic-european-health-insurance-card/
Healthcare		Access health care in other countries	https://www.nhs.uk/using-the-nhs/healthcare-abroad/healthcare-when-travelling-abroad/
Tourism for all	www.tourismforall.org.uk		
Revitalise	revitalise.org.uk		
The Disaway trust	www.disaway.co.uk		
Holidays for All	www.holidaysforall.org		
DisabledGo	www.disabledgo.com		
Mindforyou	www.mindforyou.co.uk		
Calvert Trust	www.calvert-trust.org.uk		
Holiday Home trust	www.holidayhomestrust.info		
Disabled Holiday Directory	www.disabledholidays.com		
		Foreign travel for disabled people	https://www.gov.uk/guidance/foreign-travel-for-disabled-people
Carers break in UK	https://www.carersuk.org/help-and-advice/health/looking-after-your-health/taking-a-break		

11.PALLIATIVE CARE
END OF LIFE

Created by Gregor Cresnar
from Noun Project

Checklist

Tasks	√	Tasks	√
GP			
Contact Local Hospice			
District Nurse re Sleepless nights			
Registering death			
Funeral Directors			
Bereavement payment benefit			
Planning ahead end of life			
Power of Attorney			
Advance statement			
Wills			
DNAR			

GP/Doctor surgery
Your local surgery may offer or refer you to bereavement services.
They can support you in dealing with your feelings.

Pain relief
Your local hospice will offer medical and nursing care, including
controlling pain and other symptoms.

Hospice
Hospices provide care for your loved one from the point at which
their illness is diagnosed as terminal to the end of their life, however
long that maybe.

Physiotherapy
Physiotherapy can help to restore movements and function in your
loved one if they affected by injury, illness or disability. You can ask
your loved one's GP for a referral or self-referral or pay privately.

Occupational Therapy

OT can help your loved one to improve their abilities to do everyday tasks if they are having difficulties. You can ask your loved one's GP for a referral or pay privately. Read chapter 4 Health

Complementing therapies

Hospice may offer other complementing therapies such as massage to your loved one.

Rehabilitation

Hospice maybe able to help your loved one to build their strength and health through exercise

Respite care

Hospice can provide respite. Read chapter one Respite for more information.

Financial and other practical issues

For more information, please read chapter two Finance

Bereavement care

Bereavement counsellors can offer support with discussing the funeral or other practical things if your loved one has an incurable illness, your family with the bereavement and if you are not coping with your loved one death.

Spiritual and psychological help

The hospice can assist you and your loved one with issues concerning your spiritually and psychological needs.

Night Time Respite

You can get a full night sleep a few nights a week and professional stays awake all night and cares for your loved one. If your loved one

has a terminal illness, care can be provided by Marie Curie or Macmillan. Please contact your District nurse for advice and support.

Created by Fahmihorizon
from Noun Project

Registering the death

You will need to get a death certificate from the doctor and register at the register office within 5 days. Gov.uk website explains the process from the death certificate to the funeral in a step by step guide.

Funeral Director

You and your loved one can visit the funeral director and inform them of their wishes. The funeral director will keep the information and fulfil their wishes at the relevant times. It can be one less thing to do after your loved one has died.

Bereavement benefit

Created by Gan Khoon Lay
from Noun Project

Read chapter two Finance for more information re bereavement payment benefit.

Planning ahead for end of life

Planning the end of the life with your love one can be difficult for everyone involved. It is easier to discuss everything before your loved one becomes too ill or unable to convey their wishes.

So when the time comes, you know that you are respecting your loved one's wishes.

Please look online Gov.uk, see a lawyer or citizen advice bureau before making a decision about:

Lasting Power of Attorney

"A lasting power of attorney (LPA) is a legal document that lets you (the 'donor') appoint one or more people (known as 'attorneys') to help you make decisions or to make decisions on your behalf. This gives you more control over what happens to you if you have an accident or an illness and can't make your own decisions (you 'lack mental capacity')".

Quote from www.gov.uk/power-of-attorney

Advance statement

"An advance statement lets everyone involved in your care know about your wishes, feelings and preferences if you are not able to tell them. You don't have to sign an advance statement, but your signature makes it clear that it is your wishes that have been written down."

Quote from www.nhs.uk/conditions/end-of-life-care/advance-statement

Advance decision (living will)

"An advance decision (sometimes known as an advance decision to refuse treatment, an ADRT, or a living will) is a decision you can make now to refuse a specific type of treatment at some time in the future. It lets your family, carers and health professionals know your wishes about refusing treatment if you're unable to make or communicate those decisions yourself. The treatments you're deciding to refuse must all be named in the advance decision. You may want to refuse a treatment in some situations, but not others. If this is the case, you need to be clear about all the circumstances in which you want to refuse this treatment. Deciding to refuse a treatment isn't the same as asking someone to end your life or help you end your life. *Euthanasia and assisted suicide* are illegal in England *"*

Quote from   www.nhs.uk/conditions/end-of-life-care/advance-decision-to-refuse-treatment/

Making a Will

"Your will lets you decide what happens to your money, property and possessions after your death. If you make a will you can also make sure you don't pay more Inheritance Tax than you need to."

Created by sachin modgekar from Noun Project

Quote from www.gov.uk/make-will

DNAR

"DNAR stands for Do Not Attempt Resuscitation. The DNAR form is also called a DNAR order, or DNACPR order. The information in this section applies to people living in England and Wales. What is a DNAR form? A Do Not Attempt Resuscitation form is a document issued and signed by a doctor, which tells your medical team not to attempt cardiopulmonary resuscitation (CPR). The form is designed to be easily recognised and verifiable, allowing healthcare professionals to make decisions quickly about how to treat you. It's not a legally binding document. Instead, it helps you to communicate with the healthcare professionals involved in your care that CPR shouldn't be attempted. These forms exist because without one your healthcare team will always attempt CPR. The form only covers CPR, so if you have a DNAR form you'll still be given all other types of treatment for your condition as well as treatment to ensure you're comfortable and pain-free. If you decide to have one, it's a good idea to also make an Advance Decision (Living Will) refusing CPR. This will mean that your wishes are more likely to be followed if you lack capacity to make decisions"

Quote from -https://compassionindying.org.uk/making-decisions-and-planning-your-care/planning-ahead/dnar-forms/

Find out more about planning ahead

Age UK: advance decision and advance statements
Alzheimer's Society: advance decisions and advice
Cancer research UK: advance care planning
Compassion in dying: making decisions and planning your care
Macmillan cancer support: advance care planning

Created by Hayley
from Noun Project

Contact details for more information

Association	Contact details
Local Hospice	
DNAR	Contact the local Doctor
Doctor – for death certificate	
District nurse	
Registering a death	https://www.gov.uk/after-a-death
Funeral Directors	
DWP Bereavement Support Payment	www.gov.uk/government/publications/bereavement-benefits-claim-form or order it over the phone from your local Job centre Plus
Lawyer for POA (Power of Attorney) and/or Wills	
Citizen Advice Bureau POA (Power of Attorney) and/or Wills	

12.ARMED FORCES PERSONNEL

Created by MRFA
from Noun Project

Created by Gan Khoon Lay
from Noun Project

Created by Andrejs Kirma
from Noun Project

Checklist

Tasks	√	Tasks	√
Contact the relevant association			
Contact for counselling			
Contact for financial assistance			
Contact for Equipment			
Military Funeral			

Hospital care for serving personnel

All hospital care is provided by the NHS. This include emergency and elective care. The main treatment centre for military patients seriously injured is The Royal Centre for Defence Medicine based at Queen Elizabeth Hospital Birmingham.

Non urgent and routine procedures are accessed at any NHS hospital in the UK.

The Veterans and Reserves Mental Health programme

Mental health issues relating to the service. You will need to ask the GP for a referral. If you need urgent help, please contact your GP and the local Mental health team.

Charities

General

Blesma-The limbless veterans' charity supports all Armed Forces personnel who have lost limbs, the use of limbs or their eyesight in service.

Royal British Legion provides lifelong support for the Armed Force community- serving men and women, veterans and their families.

Seafarer's Advice and Information Line-Advice service for seafarers and offer free advice on benefits, debt, housing and much more

Support/Counselling
SSAFA - lifelong emotional and practical support for active and veterans

Financial
The Soldiers' Charity -financial assistance to soldiers in need and their families. Covering debt relief, mobility assistance, education bursaries, care home fees and respite break.

The Poppy Factory is an employment charity. It support veterans of all ages and from all services in restoring their financial independence.

Practical help
Help for Heroes -direct practical support to wounded, injured and sick service personnel and veterans and family.

Hospital
Defence Medical Welfare Service (DMWS)
A charity providing practical and emotional support to military personnel, their families and other entitled civilians when they are in
hospital, rehabilitation or recovery centres.

Veterans Trauma Network
Specialist care for patients with service related traumatic injuries
If your loved one is a veteran and may benefit. Please contact Blesma, GP, Blind Veterans UK or Style for Soldiers for a referral

War Pension
To find out if you are eligible for a War pension. You will need to contact Veterans UK. They will assist and support you with the application and the lengthy process.

Funeral Military
You will need to discuss the arrangement of a military funeral with the relevant Armed Forces.

Contact details for more information

Association	Contact details
Royal British Legion	british.legion.org.uk
SSAFA-formerly Soldiers, Sailors, Airmen & Family Association	ssafa.org.uk
Help for Heroes	www.helpforheroes.org.uk/
Blesma limbless veterans	https://blesma.org/
Defence Medical Welfare Service (DMWS)	www.dmws.org.uk/
Royal Navy Benevolent Fund Trust	rnbt.org.uk
The Solders charity	soldierscharity.org
Royal Air force Association	rafa.org.uk
Royal Air force Benevolent Fund	rafbf.org
Veterans UK	veteransassociationuk.co.uk
Combat Stress	combatstress.org.uk
Bridge for heroes	www.thebridgeforheroes.org
Blind Veterans UK	www.blindveterans.org.uk/
Officers Association	www.officersassociation.org.uk
Big White wall	www.bigwhitewall.com/v2/Home.aspx
Alcoholic Anonymous	www.alcoholics-anonymous.org.uk/
Smart Recovery	https://www.smartrecovery.org.uk/
Seafarer's Advice and Information Line	sailine.org.uk
Poppy factory	www.poppyfactory.org

	Department of Community Mental health	Regional Rehabilitation Units
Aldergrove		Mil: 9491 56117 Tel: 028 944 6117
Aldershot Aldershot Centre for Health	Mil: 9243 5850 Tel: 01252335850	Mil: 94222 5722 Tel: 01252 340 722
Brize Norton	Mil: 95461 7999 Tel: 01993 897 999	

78

Bulford		Tel: 01980 672 709 Mil: 94321 2610
Catterick	Mil: 94731 3058 Tel: 01748 873 058	Mil: 94731 3786 Tel: 01748 873 786
Colchester **Army Primary Healthcare** **Service** (eastern region)	Mil: 94660 7057 Tel: 01206 817 057	Mil: 94660 7124 Tel: 0120 681 7125
Veterans and Reserve **Mental Health** **programme** DCMH Colchester	Tel: 0800 0326258 dphce-dcmhcol- vrmhp@mod.uk	
Chilwell	Mil: 94451 4450 Tel: 0115 957 4606	
Cranwell	Mil: 95751 7369 Tel: 01400 267 369	Mil: 95751 6382 Tel.: 01400 266 382
Donnington	Mil: 94480 2188 Tel: 01952 672 188	
Edinburgh		Mil: 94748 5599 Tel.: 0131 310 5599
Faslane Royal Naval Sick Quarters	Mil: 93255 5188 Tel: 01436 674 321 ext 5188	
Halton		Mil: 95237 6080 Tel: 01296 656 080
Honington		Mil: 95991 6996 Tel.: 01359 236 994
Kinloss	Tel: 01309 691 372	
Litchfield		Mil: 94422 4348 Tel: 01543 434 108
Leuchars HQ Psychiatry Scotland	Mil: 95151 7452 Tel: 01334 839 471 ext 7452	
London (Headley Court)		Tel: 01372 378 271 Mil: 95238 7290
Marham	Mil: 95951 7077 Tel: 01760 337 261 ext 7077	
Northern Ireland	Mil: 9491 61994 Tel: 028 9226 1994	

Plymouth	Mil: 9375 65965 Tel: 01752 555 965	Mil: 93756 7126 Tel: 01752 557 126
Portsmouth	Mil: 9380 26256 Tel: 02392 726 256	Mil: 9380 20847 Tel: 02392 720 842
Tidworth	Mil: 94342 2236 Tel: 01980 602 236	
Woolwich DCMH Woolwich Woolwich Station Medical centre	Mil: 94691 4363 Tel: 020 8781 4363	

INDEX

Created by H Alberto Gongora
from Noun Project

Bringing medication with overseas	62	Chiropodist	22,26 27,
Bus pass	54,58 59,64	Cinema exhibitors card	54,58 59
Calvert Trust	12,65	Cinema local	58
Care and carer assessment	10,11 14,15,	Citizen advice bureau	14,18, 19,70,7 3
Care and support plans	17,39	Coffee morning	10
Care companies	42,43	Clothes	23,54 55
Care, different types of	42,	Combat stress	78
Care home, respite	11,17 77	Commode	25
Care providers, changing	43	Complementing therapies	69
CQC	42,43	Constipation	32
Carer allowance	14,15 18	Continuing healthcare	14,17, 19
Carers break in UK	10,12 65	Continence-provisions needed for caring for your loved one	23
Carer's direct helpline	11,12	Continence nurse	25,27 30,34 36
Changing places	54,55	Council tax	14,16 19,
Charges, health	16,17 18,40	Council housing	46,47
Charities	14,18 19,76	Counselling/support	10.68,6 9,76,77
Charities, grants	14,18 19	Cream	34

Day care centre	11	Disaway trust	12,65
Deaf, how to contact 999	35,36	Discharge from hospital	38,39 42
Deaf, how to contact 111	35,36	District nurse	22-25 27,30 32-36
Deaf, Typetalk or text phone	35,36	Doctor	8,10, 12,17, 19,22 30-35 62,63 68,69 71,73
Death, registering	70,73	Domiciliary care	11,43
Defence medical welfare service	76,77, 78	DNAR	68,71 72,73
Dehydration	26,34	Dossett box	30,32
Dental services NHS	16,19, 26,27	Dressing	23,24
Dentist	16,17 22,27	Drinking	26,34
Diarrhoea	32	Duvet cover	50,51
Dietician	22,26 39	Ear drops	34
Different type of care	42	EHIC card	62,64
DisabledGo	12,65	Electricity company	14,15
Disabled Holiday directory	12,65	END OF LIFE	67
Disabled person railcard	58,59 64	English federation of disability sport	59,
Disability shops	46,47	Equipment, Household and aids, adaptions	25,47 76
Disabled taxi	58,59	Eye drops	34
Disabled toilets	54,59	Europe, how, when and where to use Blue Badge	64,

Hospital, discharge	38,39 42	Legality of a family carer	27
Hospital-non-emergency transport	38,40	Major shops-free wheelchair hire	55
Hospital stay	42	Malnourished	34
Housing benefits	47,76	Manual and positioning	22,25
Household equipment, aids and adaptions	25,47 76	Macmillan	11,18 19,69 72,
How to contact 999 for deaf people	35,36	Marie Curie	11,18 19,69
How to contact 111 for deaf people	35,36	Medication, bring with you overseas	62,
How to fold and unfold a manual wheelchair	56	Medication, stockpiling	62
How to push a manual wheelchair	56	Medication unused	30
How to put in a boot of a car	56	Mental health programme, the veterans and reserves	76,78
How to request a wheelchair or cart at the airport	63	Mindforyou	12,65
How, when and where to use blue badge in Europe	63,64	Military, funeral	76,77
Incontinence care	22,25	Mobility allowance	14,15 19,
Incontinence -provisions needed for caring for your loved one	23	Mobility car	14,15 19
Insurance, travel	62,64	Mobility equipment hire UK and Oversea	62,63 64
Lasting power of attorney	70,73	Night time respite	11,
Lawyer	70,71 73	999 nine, nine, nine	35,36

Non-emergency patient transport	38,40	Personal care- provisions	23
Nose drops	34	Personal independent payment	14,15 18
Nurse, district	22-25 27,30 32-36	Phone wet	50
Nurse, ward	38,39	Physiotherapy	30,333 6,38 39,68,
Occupational Therapist	30,33 36,38, 39,46, 47,69	Planning ahead for end of life	68,70 71
Officers Association	78	Podiatrist	22,26 27
111 one, one, one	35,36	Poppy Factory	77,78
111, how to contact for deaf people	35,36	Practical help	18,69, 77
111 online	35,36	Prescription	17,19
Optical	16,18	PROFESSIONAL CARERS	41
Optician	17,22, 26,27	Professional carers	42
Pain relief	32,68	PRN (When required)	32
PALLIATIVE CARE	67	Psychological and spiritually help	69
P.A.L.S	38-40	Radar key	54,59
Passport	62,64	Railcard, Disabled	58,59
Pension, war	17,77,	Ready meals	22,26, 27
PERSONAL CARE	21	Red Cross	54,55, 59

Refusing	31	Shopmobility	54,55 59
Registering the death	68,69 70,73	Shops, major free wheelchair hire	55
Rehabilitation	69,77, 78	Side Effects	32
Re-order	31,	Signed performance in the theatre	58
RESPITE	7	Smart recovery	78
Respite care	8,9	Social services	8,10 12,14 19,33 42,47
Respite holiday	10,12, 65	Social worker	8,10-12 15-17 19,22 25,27 38,42 43,46 47,
Respite in care homes	8,11 12	Soldiers' charity	77,78
Respite is for the carer	9	SOCIALIZING OUTSIDE THE HOME	53
Revitalise	12,65	Spare bags of clothes	54,55
Rice for a wet phone	50	Special assistance at airports in UK and abroad	63,
Royal Air Force association	78,	Sport	58,59
Royal Air Force Benevolent fund	78	Spiritual and psychological help	69
Royal British Legion	76,78	Stockpiling medication	62
Royal Navy Benevolent Fund	78	Sue Ryder	18,19
SSAFA	77,78	Support and care plans	39
Seafarer's advice & info line	77,78	Support/counselling	62,69

Support through sport	59	Unused medication	30
Sustrans	59	Urine	34,58
Swallowing problems	33,	Urine sample	34
Taxi, disabled	58	Veterans and reserves mental health programme, The	76
Telecare and alarms	46	Veterans Trauma Network	77
Telehealth systems	46	Veterans UK	77,78
Theatre, signed performance in	58	Vomiting	32
Tourism for all	65	Ward nurse	38,39
Tourist information centre	54,59	War pension	77
Train	58,59 62,64	Waste	51
Transport, non-emergency patient	38,39	Wet Shave	24
Travel charge	16,18, 40	Wheelchair, how to request a wheelchair or cart	63
Travel costs, claim	16,40	Wheelchair use	38
Travel insurance	62-64	Wheelie bin	51
Traveline	59	When required PRN	32
TRAVELLING IN THE UK AND ABROAD	61	Wigs and fabric support	17
Turn2us grant search	18,19	Will, living (advance decision)	71,72
Typetalk or textphone	35	Will, making a	71,72

Printed in Great Britain
by Amazon